Super Minds

Herbert Puchta · Peter Lewis-Jones · Günter Gerngross

Map of the Book

Friends (pages 4–9)

Vocabulary
Greetings
Numbers 1–10
Colors

Language Focus
- *What's your name? I'm Thunder.*
- *How old are you? I'm seven.*
- *Flash's bag is ...*

Story
Meet the Super Friends

Value
Making Friends

▶ **Song: Sing the Alphabet**

1 At School (pages 10–21) ❓ How do we learn?

Vocabulary
Classroom
Objects

Language Focus
- Questions and Short Answers
- Imperatives

Story
Watch Out, Flash!

Value
Helping Each Other

Phonics
The Letter Sound *a*

Skills
- Listening
- Speaking, Reading, and Writing

Think and Learn
Science: Senses

▶ **Song: What's This? What's This?** ▶ **Creativity: Create That!** ▶ **Review: Think Back**

2 Let's Play (pages 22–33) ❓ What do toys look like?

Vocabulary
Toys

Language Focus
- *What's his / her ... ?*
  How old is he / she?
- Adjectives

Story
The Go-Kart Race

Value
Fair Play: Cheating is Wrong

Phonics
The Letter Sound *e*

Skills
- Reading
- Listening, Speaking, and Writing

Think and Learn
Math: 2D Shapes

▶ **Song: Come and See** ▶ **Creativity: Do That!** ▶ **Review: Group Check**

3 Pet Show (pages 34–45) ❓ What do animals need?

Vocabulary
Animals

Language Focus
- Prepositions: *in, on, under*
- *I like / I don't like ...*

Story
The Spider

Value
Being Brave

Phonics
The Letter Sound *i*

Skills
- Listening and Speaking
- Reading, Speaking, and Writing

Think and Learn
Environmental Studies: Nature

▶ **Song: There's a Pond** ▶ **Creativity: Create That!** ▶ **Review: Think Back**

4 Lunchtime (pages 46–57) ❓ Where does food come from?

Vocabulary
Food

Language Focus
- *I have / I don't have ...*
- *Do ... have any ... ?*

Story
The Pizza

Value
Waiting Your Turn

Phonics
The Letter Sound *o*

Skills
- Listening and Writing
- Reading and Speaking

Think and Learn
Science: Food

▶ **Song: The Magic Tree** ▶ **Creativity: Do That!** ▶ **Review: Group Check**

Friends

1 🎧 01 🛡 Listen and look. Then listen and say the words.

2 Thunder
4 Flash
1 Whisper
3 Misty

2 🎧 02 Listen and chant.

Hi, I'm Whisper.
What's your name?
Hi, I'm Thunder.
What a nice name!

Hi, I'm Flash.
What's your name?
Hi, I'm Misty.
What a nice name!

4 Greetings

1 🎧 03 Listen and point to the numbers.

2 🎧 04 How old are the Super Friends? Listen and write.

I'm _____.

I'm _____.

I'm _____.

I'm _____.

3 Ask and answer.

Numbers

1 🎧 05 ▶ **Listen and sing.**

A B C D E
F G H I J
Hey! Sing with me!
K L M N O
P Q R S T
Sing with me.
U V W X Y Z
We can sing the alphabet!
We can sing the alphabet!

2 🛡 **Play the alphabet game.**

1 🎧07 Listen and point to the balloons.

2 🎧08 Listen and match.

3 Look at Activity 2. Make sentences.

Flash's bag is …

Meet the Super Friends

   What is the cat's name?

Misty, Whisper, and Flash: Wow!

Flash: Look at me!
Thunder, Misty, and Whisper: Cool!

Misty: My turn. Look!

Thunder, Whisper, and Flash: Misty?

Misty: What about you, Whisper?
Whisper: I speak to animals.

Whisper: What's your name, cat?
Cat: I'm Tabby.

 Value: Making Friends

Thunder: Wow! How old are you?
Cat: Meow.

Whisper: No! Listen to me.

Whisper: How old are you?
Cat: I'm four.

Thunder, Misty, and Flash: Cool.

2 Read and number the pictures

1. Look at me.
2. My turn. Look!
3. I'm Tabby.
4. How old are you?
5. No! Listen to me.

Listening and Reading 9

1 At School

1 🎧 10 🛡 Listen and look. Then listen and say the words.

1 ruler
2 pen
3 book
4 eraser
5 pencil case
6 pencil
7 desk
8 notebook
9 bag
10 paper

BIG QUESTION How do we learn?

2 🎧 11 Listen and chant.

Flash, Flash, please come back!
Flash, Flash, please come back!

Your ruler, your pen,
Your paper, your book,
Your pencil,
And your pencil case.

Flash, Flash, close your bag!
Flash, Flash, close your bag!

Your ruler, your pen,
Your paper, your book,
Your pencil,
And your pencil case.

10 Classroom Objects

1. 🎧 12 **Listen and number the pictures.**

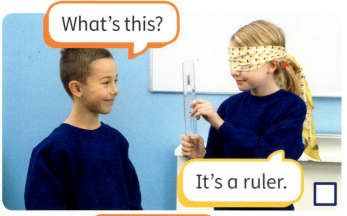

2. ▶ 🎧 13 **Watch, listen, and say.**

Language Focus

What's this?

Is it a pencil?   **Is it a** ruler?
No, **it isn't**.   Yes, **it is**.

3. **Play the guessing game.**

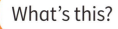

Questions and Short Answers 11

1 🎧 14 ▶ **Listen and sing. Then check ✓ the objects in the song.**

What's this? What's this?
Please tell me, what's this?
Is it a pen? Is it a book?
Come on, take a look.

It's a pencil, it's a pencil,
A pencil for my school.
It's a pencil, it's a pencil,
And the pencil's very cool.

What's this? What's this? ...

It's a notebook, it's a notebook,
A notebook for my school.
It's a notebook, it's a notebook,
And the notebook's very cool.

2 **Check ✓ the objects that are for school.**

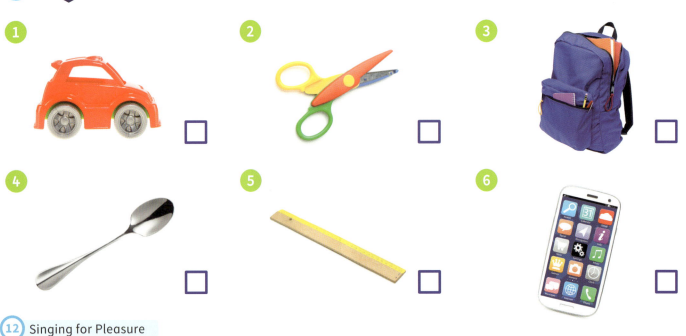

Singing for Pleasure

1 🎧 16   Listen and stick. Then write the words.

pen   book   bag   desk

1. Sit at your _____, please.
2. Open your _____, please.
3. Close your _____, please.
4. Pass me a _____, please. Here you go.

2 ▶ 🎧 17 Watch, listen, and say.

Language Focus

Sit at your desk, please.   **Open** your book, please.
Now **get** a pen.   **Write** one to ten.

3 Play the please game.

Open your book.

Open your book, please.

Imperatives 13

Watch Out, Flash!

   Which classroom objects can you see?

Store Manager: Pass me the box, please.

Delivery Man: Watch out!

Flash: I'm sorry.
Delivery Man: It's OK.

Flash: Mom! My notebook!
Mom: Here you go!

Flash: Thank you.
Mom: Flash, come back!

Thunder: Here's your pencil case.
Whisper: Here's your ruler.
Misty: Here's your book.

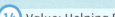

Flash: Oh, no!
Thunder: What is it?

Flash: My bag!

2 Find these things in the story.

a is in picture …

Phonics

3 Find who says …

*My b**a**g!*

4 🎧 19 Listen and say.

Come b**a**ck, M**a**tt! Here's your bl**a**ck b**a**g!

Phonics: The Letter Sound *a*

Skills

1 🎧 20 **Listen and draw lines.**

Sam   Fred   Kim

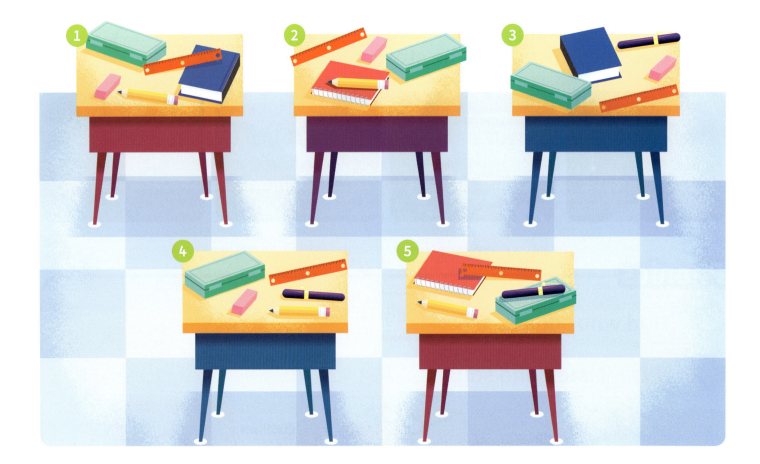

Mia   Jane

1 Ask and answer.

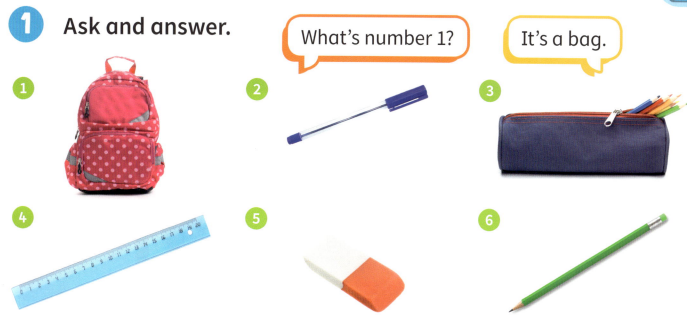

What's number 1?   It's a bag.

2 Read and draw lines.

1. Put away your book, please.
2. Take out your ruler, please.
3. Pass me a pencil, please.
4. Open your bag, please.

3 Make a question card. Then play the guessing game.

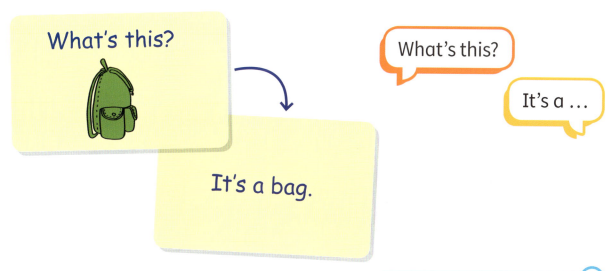

What's this?

What's this?

It's a ...

It's a bag.

Speaking, Reading, and Writing

Think and Learn

Senses

▶ **How do we learn?**

1 🎧 21 **Listen and point.**

look

listen

smell

taste

touch

2 Which senses do you use? Read and check ✓.

	look	listen	smell	taste	touch
1 Listen to a story.					
2 Open your pencil case.					
3 Eat your lunch.					
4 Close your bag.					
5 Watch a video.					

18 Science

3 Read and complete the pictures.

In picture 1, Flash looks at something.

In picture 2, Flash smells something.

In picture 3, Flash tastes something.

4 ⭐ Project Make a senses book.

look   listen   touch   taste   smell

Science 19

Create That!

1   Listen and imagine. Then draw your picture.

2 Work with a partner. Compare your pictures.

What's this?   It's a …

20 Creativity

Think Back 1

1 Read and circle.

1. It's a …

   a pencil.   b ruler.   c desk.

2. It's a …
   a pen.   b pencil case.   c notebook.

3. … your book, please.
   a Open   b Close   c Pass me

4. … at your desk, please.

   a Sit   b Write   c Take out

5. Is this a pencil case?
   a Yes, it is.   b No, it isn't.

6. Is this a bag?

   a Yes, it is.   b No, it isn't.

7. This is Flash's …
   a pencil case.   b box.   c ruler.

8. You … a song.

   a look at   b listen to   c smell

Review 21

2 Let's Play

1 🎧 23 **Listen and look. Then listen and say the words.**

1. computer game
2. kite
3. plane
4. bike
5. doll
6. monster
7. train
8. go-kart
9. car
10. ball

BIG QUESTION What do toys look like?

2 🎧 24 **Listen and chant.**

Open the door, come with me.
Lots of toys for you and me.
A doll, a car, a monster, and a train,
A big, big ball, a go-kart, and a plane.

Open the door, come with me.
Lots of toys for you and me.
A bike, a kite, and a computer game.
A big, big ball, a go-cart, and a plane.

22 Toys

1   Listen and stick.

Sophie   Alex   Olivia   Mark

2   Watch, listen, and say.

Language Focus

What's **his** name?
His name's Ben.
How old is **he**?
He's ten.
What's **his** favorite toy?
His favorite toy's **his** train.

What's **her** name?
Her name's Kate.
How old is **she**?
She's eight.
What's **her** favorite toy?
Her favorite toy's **her** plane.

3 Ask and answer.

What's his name?

How old is he?

What's his / her … ? How old is he / she?

1 ▶ **Listen and sing. Then draw lines to the toys in the song.**

Hello, come and see me.
Hello, meet my friends.
This is Mike and this is Jane.
Come and see my friends.

How old is he?
What's his name?
What's his favorite toy?
He's seven years old.
His name's Mike.
His favorite toy's his bike.

Hello, come and see me …

How old is she?
What's her name?
What's her favorite toy?
She's seven years old.
Her name's Jane.
Her favorite toy's her plane.

Hello, come and see me …

2 **Write a new verse for the song.**

She's _____

Her name's _____

Her favorite toy's _____

24 Singing for Pleasure

1 🎧29 **Listen and number the pictures.**

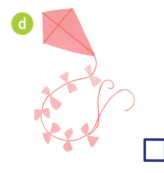

a. A big blue plane.
b. A small orange plane.
c. An ugly black kite.
d. A beautiful pink kite.
e. A long yellow train.
f. A short green train.
g. An old pink bike.
h. A new purple bike.

2 ▶ 🎧30 **Watch, listen, and say.**

Language Focus

It's a **white** ball.   It's an **ugly** ball.
It's a **big white** ball.   And it's **cold**.

The desk is different. It is new.

3 🛡 **Find the different picture and say.**

Adjectives 25

The Go-Kart Race

   Why is Misty happy?

Man: This is Ben from the Red team, and this is Misty from the Green team!
Red team driver: Ha ha ha! What an ugly old go-kart!

Man: 1, 2, 3—go!
Thunder and Whisper: Go!

Flash: Great, Misty!
Red team girl: She's first! Stop her!

Misty: Help!
Thunder: Oh, no!
Red team driver: Ha ha ha! Now I'm first!

Misty: That isn't fair!
Thunder: Just a minute.

Thunder: Hold on, Misty!

 Value: Fair Play

Misty: Whoa!
Red team driver: No!

Man: Congratulations, Misty! You're first!
Misty: Thank you!

2 Look at the picture and check ✓ the correct sentence.

1 Congratulations! ☐
2 Help! ☐
3 Hold on. ☐
4 Just a minute. ☐

Phonics

3 Find who says …

This is B**e**n from the r**e**d team!

4 🎧 32 Listen and say.

K**e**n and his t**e**n r**e**d p**e**ns!

Phonics: The Letter Sound e

Skills

1 Look at the pictures and choose the correct words.

①

It's **a big** / **a small** ball.

②

It's **an ugly** / **a beautiful** monster.

③

It's **a long** / **a short** train.

④

It's **a small** / **a big** car.

⑤

It's **a beautiful** / **an ugly** doll.

⑥

It's **a new** / **an old** teddy bear.

1 🎧 33 Listen and draw lines.

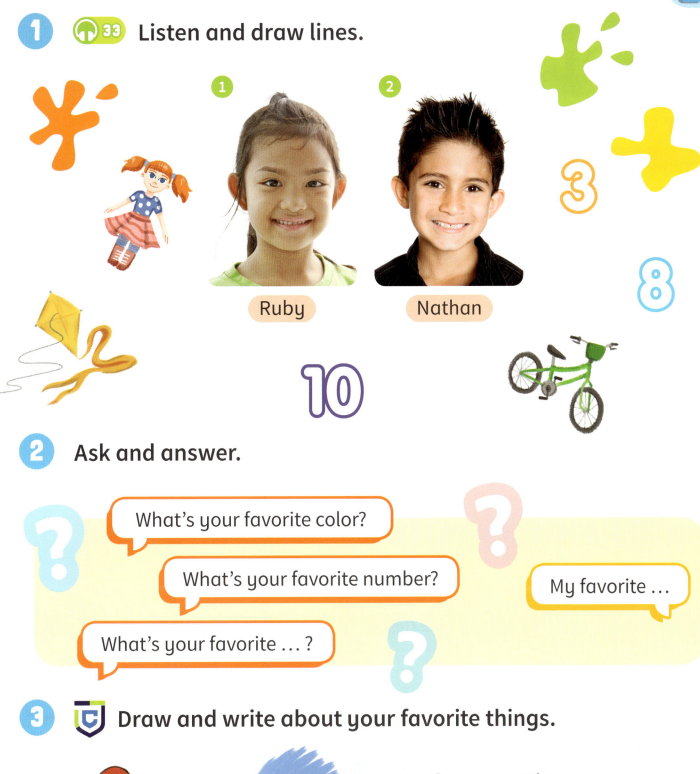

Ruby   Nathan

2 Ask and answer.

- What's your favorite color?
- What's your favorite number?
- What's your favorite … ?
- My favorite …

3 Draw and write about your favorite things.

My Favorite Things
My favorite color is blue.
My favorite number is nine.
My favorite toy is my doll.

Listening, Speaking, and Writing 29

Think and Learn

2D Shapes

▶ What toys do you know?   **1** 🎧 34 Listen and point.

1. triangle   2. circle   3. kite   4. square   5. rectangle

2   Look at Activity 1. Read and match.

1 The triangle is …   a red.

2 The circle is …   b yellow.

3 The kite is …   c orange.

4 The square is …   d brown.

5 The rectangle …   e green.

3   Look and draw the next shapes. Then describe the shapes.

1    A small blue circle, a big …

2

3

30 Math

4 Ask and answer.

1 Which shapes are in the toys?

The train.

Two circles and a rectangle.

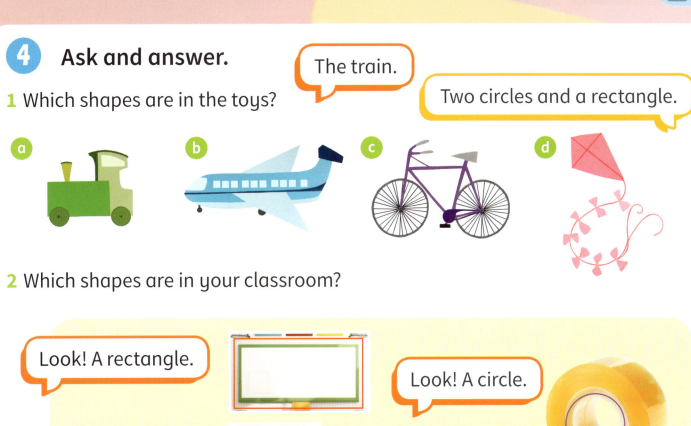

2 Which shapes are in your classroom?

Look! A rectangle.

Look! A circle.

Look! A square.

5 Project — Design a toy and write.

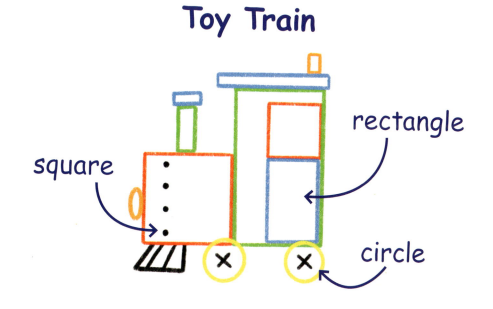

Toy Train

square
rectangle
circle

Do That!

1 🎧 35 Listen and act it out with your teacher. Then listen again and number the pictures.

2 Read the sentences from the story and draw lines.

a Fly the plane. ●   ● b Ouch!

c Take a piece of paper. ●   ● d It's a plane!

e Fold the piece of paper. ●   ● f Where's the plane?

3 Listen to a friend and act out the instructions.

Take a piece of paper.

Cut the paper.

It's a kite!

32 Creativity

Group Check Units 1 and 2

1 How many words can you remember? Draw pictures.

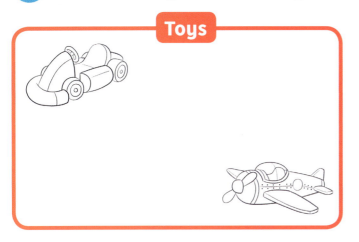

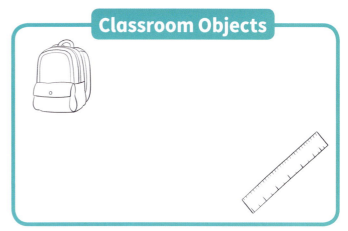

2 Write and say the words.

3 🎧 36 Listen and number.

His name's Rory. ☐

It's a monster. ☐

What's his name? ☐

What's this? ☐

4 Write a new dialogue. Act it out.

What's this?

It's _____.

_____ name?

_____.

Review 33

3 Pet Show

1 🎧 37 Listen and look. Then listen and say the words.

1 donkey
2 elephant
3 spider
4 cat
5 rat
6 frog
7 duck
8 lizard
9 dog

BIG QUESTION What do animals need?

2 🎧 38 Listen and chant.

Pet show, pet show,
Look at all the pets.

Whisper and his spider,
Daisy and her dog,
Lenny and his lizard,
Sandra and her frog.

Donnie and his duck,
Katie and her cat,
Thunder and his elephant,
Misty and her rat.

Pet show, pet show,
Look at all the pets …

34 Animals

Listen and stick.

   Watch, listen, and say.

Language Focus

The frog's **in** my bag.
It's **under** my chair.
The frog's **on** my hat.
It's really there.

My frog? Where is it?
It's not **in** my bag.
It's not **under** my chair.
It's not **on** my hat.
It isn't there.

Play the description game.

The cat …

Number …

Prepositions: *in, on, under*

Listen and sing. Then check ✓ the animals in the song.

The frog's on a bag,
And that's not good.
Put the frog in the pond,
Yes, the pond in the woods.

**There's a pond, there's a pond
There's a pond in the woods.
There's a pond in the woods,
And that's good!**

The duck's under the car,
And that's not good.
Put the duck in the pond,
Yes, the pond in the woods.

There's a pond, there's a pond ...

The fish is in the net,
And that's not good.
Put the fish in the pond,
Yes, the pond in the woods.

There's a pond, there's a pond ...

  Look, think, and draw.

Which animals need a pond?

Need a Pond	Don't Need a Pond

36 Singing for Pleasure; There's a Pond

1 🎧 43 Listen and circle what the spider says.

2 ▶ 🎧 44 Watch, listen, and say.

> **Language Focus**
>
> I **like** frogs.　　　Croak, croak!
> What about you?　　I **don't like big** frogs!
> I **like** frogs, too.　Croak. Croak!

3 Ask and answer.

I like … What about you?

I …

I like / I don't like …

The Spider

1   Where's the spider in picture 3?

Whisper: Come back. He's beautiful. Look!
Flash: Oh, no. I don't like spiders.

Whisper: Touch him, Misty.
Misty: Wow!

Whisper: Look, he's under the table.

Flash: He's smart.
Thunder: He's amazing.

Misty: I like spiders.
Flash: They're great.

Spider: They like spiders! I have an idea.
Whisper: What?

Value: Being Brave

Spider: My brothers and sisters are on the tree!

Whisper: Oh, no!
Misty, Flash, and Thunder: Aagh!

2 Read and circle *yes* or *no*.

1 In picture one, Flash and Whisper like the spider. yes / no
2 In picture three, the spider is under the table. yes / no
3 In picture four, the spider is smart. yes / no
4 In picture eight, Misty, Thunder, and Flash like the spiders. yes / no

Phonics

3 Find who says …   Touch h**i**m, M**i**sty.

4 🎧 46 Listen and say.

Th**is is** T**i**m and h**is** s**i**lly s**i**ster K**i**m.

Phonics: The Letter Sound *i*

Skills

1   Listen and stick.

2 Look and say.

The cat's …

40 Listening and Speaking

1 Read and circle the correct picture.

Pet Show

Come to the pet show. See two dogs, two lizards, four cats, two big spiders, and two donkeys!

2 Look at Activity 1. Make sentences.

There are eight dogs.

3 Make a poster.

Animals

I like spiders and lizards.

My favorite animals are cats!

I don't like rats.

Think and Learn

▶ **What do animals drink?**

1 🎧 48 **Listen and point.**

shelter

food

water

air

2 Look at the animals in Activity 1 and write.

1 The dog needs _____.   3 The bird needs _____.

2 The spider needs _____.   4 The cat needs _____.

3 Look and say *food*, *water*, or *shelter*.   Picture 1.   Food.

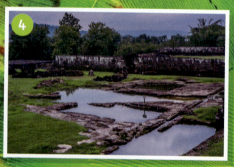

Environmental Studies

4 Look and say.

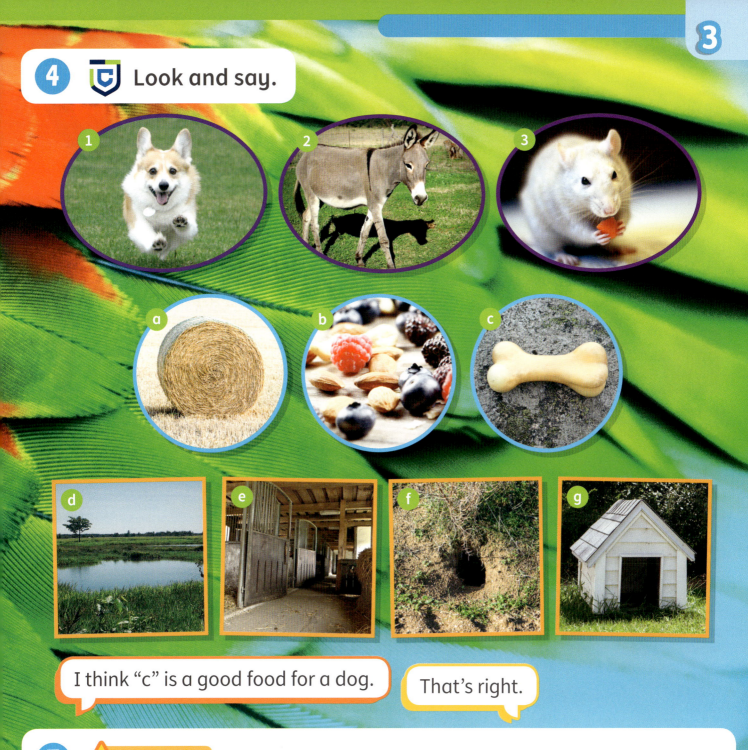

I think "c" is a good food for a dog.

That's right.

5 Project — Make a spiderweb.

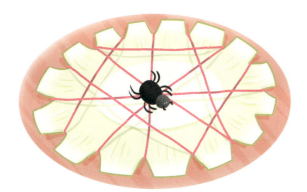

My spider lives in a ... for shelter. It eats ... . It drinks ... .

Environmental Studies

Create That!

1   Listen and imagine. Then draw your picture.

2 Work with a partner. Compare your pictures.

- The animal in my picture is …
- In your picture, there's …

44 Creativity

Think Back 3

1 Read and circle.

1 This is a …
   a lizard.   b donkey.   c cat.

2 This is a …
   a rat.   b frog.   c spider.

3 The lizard is … the desk.
   a on   b in   c under

4 The duck is … the pond.
   a on   b in   c under

5 I … spiders.
   a like   b don't like

6 I … cats.
   a like   b don't like

7 In the story, … pet is a spider.
   a Thunder's   b Misty's   c Whisper's

8 This is … for the duck.
   a food   b water   c shelter

Review 45

4 Lunchtime

1 🎧 50 Listen and look. Then listen and say the words.

1. apple
2. banana
3. cake
4. pizza
5. sausage
6. cheese sandwich
7. fish
8. chicken
9. peas
10. steak
11. carrots

BIG QUESTION Where does food come from?

2 🎧 51 Listen and chant.

Lunchtime! Lunchtime!
What's for lunch?

I don't like chicken,
And I don't like cheese.
I don't like pizza,
And I don't like peas.

Lunchtime! Lunchtime!
What's for lunch?

Oh, I like apples,
And I like steak.
Oh, I like carrots,
And I like cake!
Yummy!

46 Food

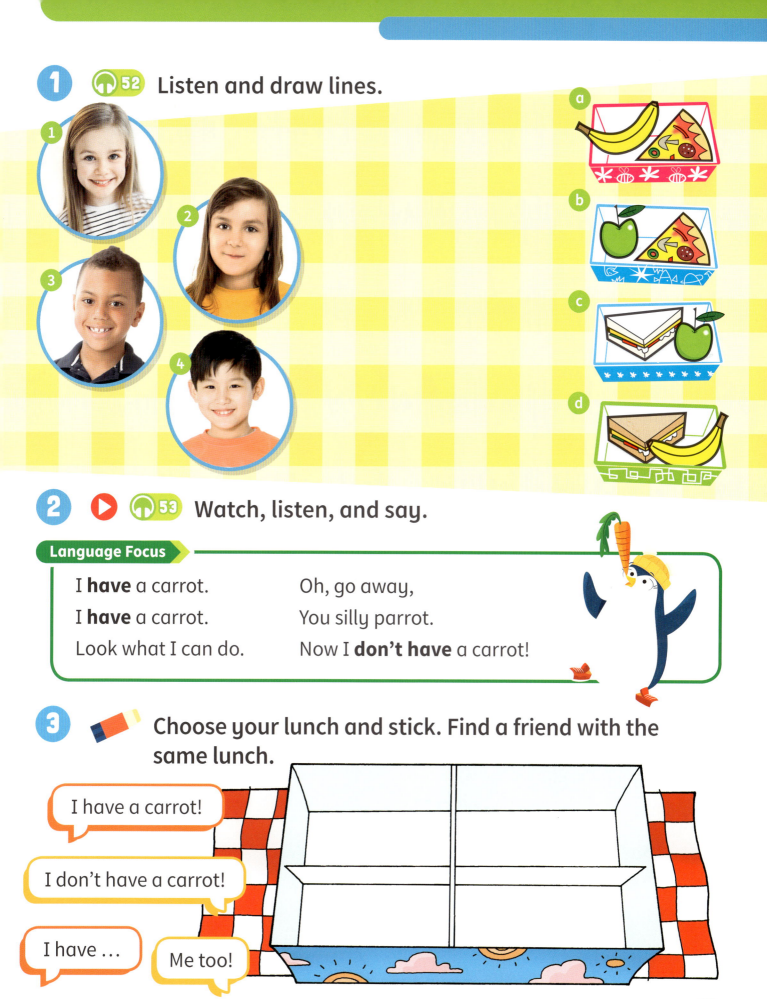

1   Listen and sing. Then check ✓ the food in the song.

I have a magic tree
With lots of things to eat.
I have a magic tree.
Let's go and get a treat.

Pick an ice cream cone from the tree.
Pick an orange from the tree.
Pick an apple from the tree.
It's there for you and me.

I have a magic tree
With lots of things to take.
I have a magic tree.
Let's go and get a cake.

Pick an ice cream cone from the tree ...

2 Look, think, and write.

Which Food Grows on Trees?

on the magic tree → ice cream cone

on real trees ←

↑ on the magic tree and on real trees

48 Singing for Pleasure; The Magic Tree

1 Follow the lines. Read and check ✓.

1 Do we have any cheese?
   ☐ Yes, we do.
   ☐ No, we don't.

2 Do we have any orange juice?
   ☐ Yes, we do.
   ☐ No, we don't.

3 Do we have any sausages?
   ☐ Yes, we do.
   ☐ No, we don't.

4 Do we have any fish?
   ☐ Yes, we do.
   ☐ No, we don't.

2   56 Watch, listen, and say.

Language Focus

Penny, I'm hungry.
Do we **have any** fish?
No, we **don't**.
We don't have any fish.

Penny, I'm hungry.
Do we **have any** fish?
Yes, we **do**!
Yes, we have a fish!

3 Ask and answer.

Do we have any pizza?

Yes, we do.

Do … have any … ?

The Pizza

   Which food can you see in picture 8?

Thunder: Where's Misty?

Misty: Mmm … pizza. My favorite!

Whisper: Look at Misty!
Flash: Hey! That isn't fair.

Misty: Pizza, please.
Woman: Sorry. We don't have pizza.

Misty: OK. Sausages and peas, please.

Woman: Here you go.
Misty: Thank you.

50 Value: Waiting Your Turn

Thunder: Look!
Woman: A new pizza. Nice and hot.
Flash: Fantastic!

Misty: What do you have?
Whisper, Thunder, and Flash: We have pizza. Nice and hot!

2 Read and check ✓ or write an ✗.

Who says … ?				
I have pizza.				
I have an apple.				
I have sausages.				
I have peas.				
I have a banana.				

Phonics

3 Find who says …   *Sorry, we don't have pizza.*

4 🎧58 Listen and say.

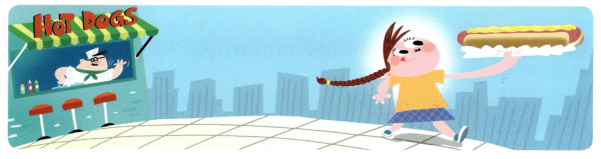

P**o**lly st**o**ps at the sh**o**p f**o**r a h**o**t d**o**g.

Phonics: The Letter Sound o

Skills

1 🎧 59 Listen and say the numbers.

eleven — twelve — thirteen — fourteen — fifteen
sixteen — seventeen — eighteen — nineteen — twenty

2 🎧 60 Listen and write.

In the Fridge
_____ carrots
13 _____
1 _____
_____ sausages

3 What's in your fridge? Think and write.

In My Fridge
14 pizzas

1 Look, read, and circle the five mistakes in the texts.

Noah: I have twelve sausages and two cheese sandwiches. I don't have any steaks. I have a chicken.

Peter: I have thirteen apples. I don't have a cake. I don't have a pizza.

Emily: I have three bananas and twelve carrots. I don't have four fish. I don't have a chicken.

2 Make a shopping list for a school lunch.

We need twelve bananas, …

Reading and Speaking

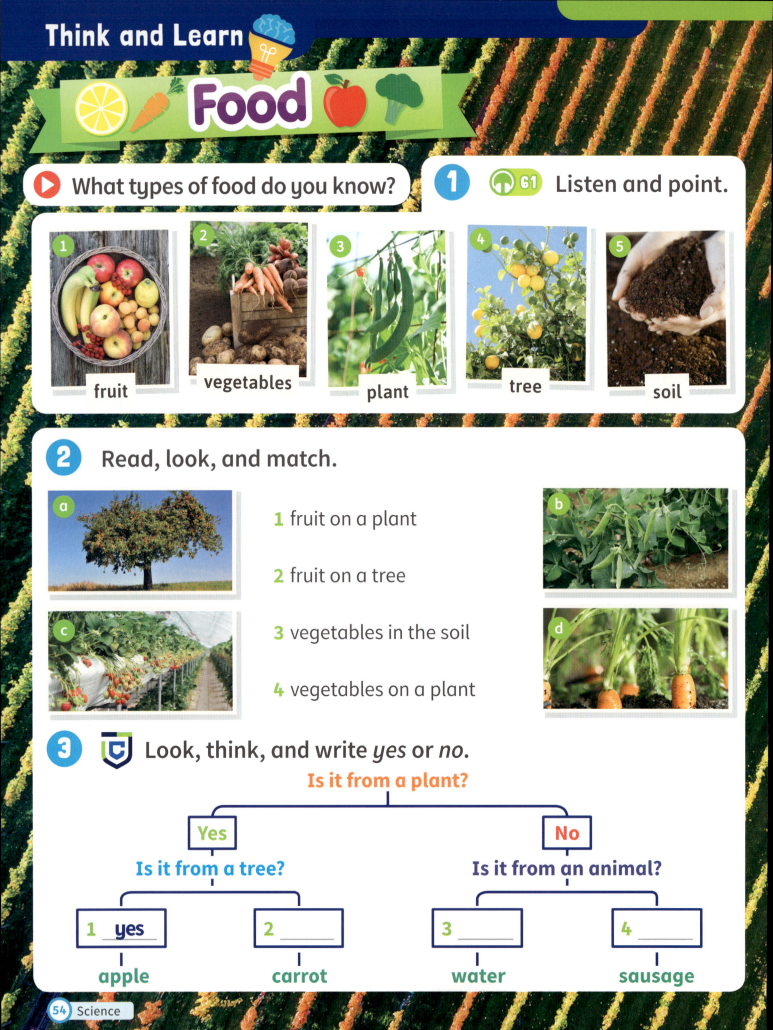

4   Look, read, and write the numbers.

1 The potato is in the soil.
2 Now it's a big potato.
3 The potato is in a store.
4 It's lunchtime! The potato is in a salad. Yum!

5   Project   Write a story about a fruit.

The Story of a Banana

The banana is on the tree.

Now it's a big banana.

The banana is in a store.

It's breakfast. I eat the banana. Yum!

Do That!

1 🎧 62 Listen and act it out with your teacher. Then listen again and number the pictures.

2 Read the sentences from the story and draw lines.

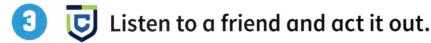

a Buy a banana.　　　　　　　　b You slip on the banana peel. Ouch!

c Eat the banana.　　　　　　　　d Go out of the store.

e Throw the peel down!　　　　　f You are hungry.

3 🛡 Listen to a friend and act it out.

Buy fifteen chickens.

Eat the chickens.

You have a stomachache. Ouch!

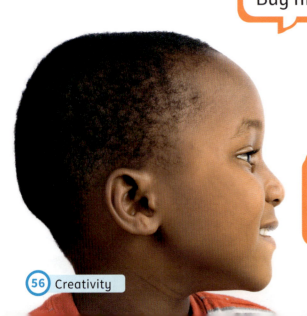

Group Check Units 3 and 4 4

1 How many words can you remember? Draw pictures.

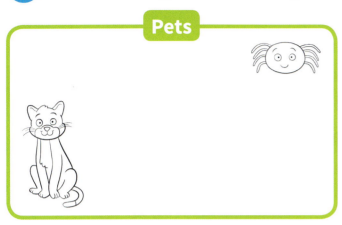

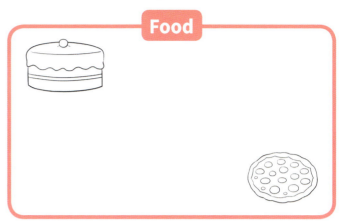

2 Write and say the words.

3 🎧 63 Listen and number.

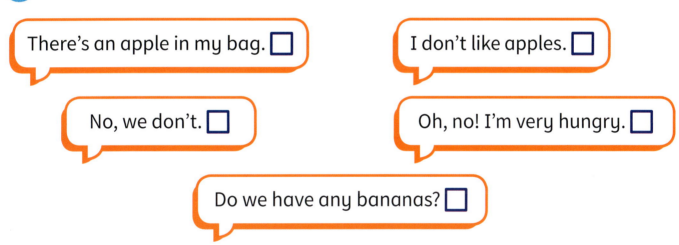

There's an apple in my bag. ☐

I don't like apples. ☐

No, we don't. ☐

Oh, no! I'm very hungry. ☐

Do we have any bananas? ☐

4 🛡 Write a new dialogue. Act it out.

💬 Do we have _____?

💬 No, _____.

💬 Oh, no! I'm very hungry.

💬 There's _____ in my _____.

💬 I _____.

Review 57

5 Free Time

1 🎧 64 　 Listen and look. Then listen and say the words.

BIG QUESTION Which activities do we do?

2 🎧 65 　 Listen and chant.

Monday and Tuesday
Are fantastic days!
Wednesday and Thursday
Are fantastic days!

Friday and Saturday
Are fantastic days!
But Sunday's the best.
We just play and rest!

58　Days of the Week

1   Listen and stick.

Sandra	Pat	Maria	Oliver	Bill

2 Watch, listen, and say.

Language Focus

I **go swimming** on Mondays,
Swimming in the ocean.
I **play soccer** on Tuesdays.
Come and play with me!

I **go fishing** on Wednesdays,
On Thursdays and Fridays, too.
But on Saturdays and Sundays,
I like **being** with you!

3 Play the true or false game.

I go flying on Sundays.

That's false.

Yes, it is.

I (watch TV) on (Sundays).

Listen and sing. Then write the days.

I'm bored. I'm bored.
I have nothing to do!
I'm bored. I'm bored.
What can I do with you?

On Mondays, I play board games.
On Tuesdays, I kick my soccer ball.
On Wednesdays, I play tennis.
On Thursdays, I play them all!

I'm bored. I'm bored …

On Fridays, I go swimming.
On Saturdays, I sing songs.
On Sundays, I ride my bike.
Why don't you come along?
Please come along.

2 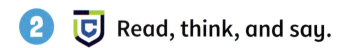 **Read, think, and say.**

How are you the same as the girl in the song? What do you do?

On Mondays, I play board games.

1 🎧 70 Listen and check ✓ or put an ✗.

2 ▶ 🎧 71 Watch, listen, and say.

> **Language Focus**
>
> **Do you watch** TV on the weekend?
> No, I **don't**.
> **Do you play** computer games?
> Yes, I **do**.
>
> **Do you ride** your horse on the weekend?
> No, I **don't**.
> **Do you ride** your bike with Paul?
> Yes, I **do**.

3 Play the find someone game.

On the weekend, …
I play tennis _____ with my friend.
I sing _____.
I go swimming _____.

Do you sing on the weekend?

Yes, I do.

Do you … ? Yes, I do. / No, I don't.

We're Lost!

  Which pictures is the rabbit in?

Misty: Where's the lake?
Flash: I don't know.
Thunder: We're lost!

Whisper: I have an idea.
Flash: What?

Whisper: Wait and see.
Thunder: This isn't much fun.

Whisper: Rabbit, we're lost. Where's the lake?
Rabbit: Come with me.

Whisper: Thank you very much.
Thunder: Here you go, rabbit.

Rabbit: Yippee!
Whisper: Watch out!

 Value: Asking for Help When You Need It

Whisper: Are you OK, Rabbit?

Rabbit: Now, I'm lost!
Whisper: Now, he's lost!

2 Look at the picture and check ✓ the correct sentence.

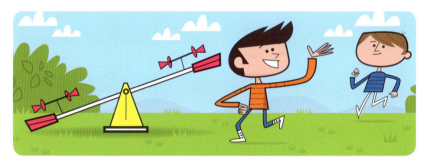

1 Are you OK? ☐
2 Come with me. ☐
3 Here you go. ☐
4 I'm lost! ☐

Phonics

3 Find who says …   This isn't m**u**ch f**u**n.

4 🎧73 Listen and say.

On S**u**ndays, Mom has f**u**n with the d**u**cks in the m**u**d.

Phonics: The Letter Sound *u*

Skills

1   Listen and stick.

	Monday	Tuesday	Wednesday	Thursday	Friday	Saturday	Sunday
Jim							
Emily							

2 Ask and answer.

Do you ride your bike on Saturdays?

Do you play with your friends on Sundays?

	✓ Yes, I do.	✗ No, I don't.
Do you ride your bike on Saturdays?		
Do you play board games on Saturdays?		
Do you go swimming on Saturdays?		
Do you play with your toys on Sundays?		
Do you watch TV on Sundays?		
Do you play with your friends on Sundays?		

1 Read the poem and check ✓ the pictures.

My Perfect Week

On Mondays,
I play soccer.

On Tuesdays,
I ride my bike.

On Wednesdays,
I play tennis.

On Thursdays,
I go swimming.

On Fridays,
I play board games.

On Saturdays and Sundays,
I watch TV and sleep.

That's my perfect week.

2 Write a poem about your perfect week.

My perfect week
On Mondays, I play
with my friends.

Think and Learn

Activities

▶ **What do we do?**

1 🎧 75 **Listen and point.**

go skiing

go surfing

go climbing

go running

go sledding

2 Look at the photos in Activity 1. Ask and answer.

What do they do in picture 1?

They go skiing.

3 🛡 **Look, think, and write.**

go skiing   go surfing   go climbing   go running   go sledding   go swimming

_____   _____   _____
_____   _____   _____

4 🎧 76 **Listen and check.**

66 Physical Education

5 Look and say.

> We play soccer in picture 3.

> We don't play soccer in picture 4.

6  Make a poster.

> I like soccer. I don't like surfing.

Physical Education

Create That!

1   Listen and imagine. Then draw your picture.

2 Work with a partner. Compare your pictures.

On my perfect Sunday, I …

On your perfect Sunday, you …

68 Creativity

Think Back 5

1 Read and circle.

1 The day after Monday is …
   a Sunday.   b Wednesday.   c Tuesday.

2 The day before Friday is …
   a Monday.   b Thursday.   c Saturday.

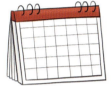

3 I … on Tuesdays.
   a go fishing   b ride my horse   c play tennis

4 I … on Fridays.
   a watch TV   b go swimming   c play soccer

5 Do you sing songs on the weekend?
   a Yes, I do.   b No, I don't.

6 Do you ride your bike on the weekend?
   a Yes, I do.   b No, I don't.

7 In the story, the Super Friends see a …
   a frog.   b rabbit.   c rat.

8 On Mondays, I …
   a go skiing.   b go climbing.   c go running.

Review 69

6 The Old House

1 🎧 78 Listen and look. Then listen and say the words.

1. bedroom
2. bathroom
3. living room
4. kitchen
5. hall
6. stairs
7. basement
8. dining room

BIG QUESTION How are houses different?

2 🎧 79 Listen and chant.

Let's go to the scary house,
The scary house, the scary house.
Let's go to the scary house,
Let's go in!

What's in the bedroom?
What's in the bathroom?
What's in the basement?
Let's go and see!

Let's go to the scary house,
The scary house, the scary house.
Let's go to the scary house,
Let's go in!

What's in the dining room?
What's in the living room?
What's in the kitchen?
Let's go and see!

70 The House

1 🎧 80 **Listen and match the monsters with their bedrooms.**

2 ▶ 🎧 81 **Watch, listen, and say.**

Language Focus

There's a fish in the hall
And two fish in the living room.

There are three fish in the kitchen.
There are four fish in the dining room.

3 **Play the description game.**

In this picture, there's a …

 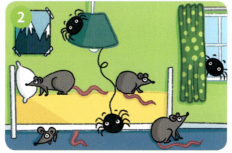 

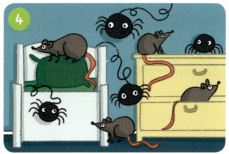  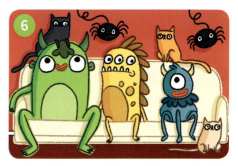

There's / There are … 71

1   Listen and sing. Then look and draw lines.

We live in different houses you and me
Me and you, you and me.
We live in different houses you and me.
You live in an apartment
And I live in a tree!

Some people live in houses,
Some people live in cars,
Some people live in apartments,
Or in tents under the stars.

We live in different houses ...

Some houses are very old,
Some houses are new,
Some houses are very small,
Some have beautiful views.

We live in different houses ...

2 Ask and answer.

Which house is your favorite?

My favorite house is ...

72 Singing for Pleasure; We Live in Different Houses

1   Listen, look, and stick.

1 Is there a park?	
2 Are there any bikes?	
3 Are there any dogs?	
4 How many ducks are there?	

2   Watch, listen, and say.

Language Focus

Is there a park? **Are there any** trees?
No, **there isn't**. No, **there aren't**.
Is there a school? **Are there any** houses?
Yes, **there is**. Yes, **there are**.
  How many are there?

3 Look at Activity 1 again. Ask and answer.

Is there a … ?

Yes, there is.

At the House

1 🎧 86 ▶ Which animals can you see in picture 8?

Misty: There's the old house. Let's go in.
Flash: Go in? No way!

Misty: OK. Let me go in. Wait for me here.
Thunder: Careful, Misty.

Misty: The stairs to the basement! How many are there?

Misty: It's cold here. What's this?

Misty: Yuck! Big spiders!

Misty: Wow! Big rats!

74 Value: Taking Care of Your Friends

Misty: There's no problem. You can come in.
Whisper: Misty, where are you?

Misty: Here I am.
Thunder: Help!
Flash and Whisper: Aagh!

2 Make sentences with a friend.

In picture one, there's a house.

In picture five, there are twelve spiders.

Phonics

3 Find who says ... **H**elp!

4 🎧 87 Listen and say.

In **H**arry's **h**ouse, there's a **h**airy spider.

Phonics: The Letter Sound *h*

Skills

1 🎧 88 **Listen and write the numbers.**

How many are there?

1 living rooms: _____

2 bathrooms: _____

3 kitchens: _____

4 bedrooms: _____

5 yards: _____

6 dining rooms: _____

2 **Write about your house.**

There are two bedrooms, a living room, a kitchen, and a hall.

I live in a house.

There's a yard.

I like my house. It's beautiful!

1 Look, read, and write *a*, *b*, *c*, or *d*.

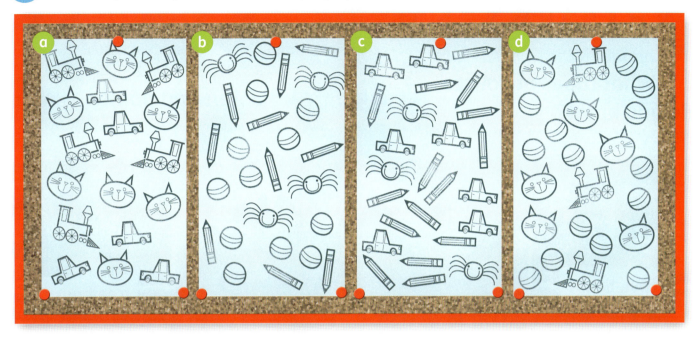

1 There are fifteen pencils. ☐
2 There are five trains. ☐
3 There are seven cars. ☐
4 There are four spiders. ☐
5 There are fourteen balls. ☐
6 There are six cats. ☐

2 Look at Activity 1 again. Ask and answer.

How many trains are there in picture d?

There are three.

Think and Learn
Houses

▶ What types of houses do you know?

1 🎧 89 Listen and point.

cave house

houseboat

tree house

yurt

2 Cover the photos in Activity 1. Ask and answer.

What's picture 1?   It's a cave house.

3 Look at Activity 1 again. Read and answer.

Which house …

1 is on water? _____

2 is round? _____

3 has stairs in it? _____

4 is small and in a tree? _____

78 Geography

4 Look at the pictures. Ask and answer.

1 What houses are they?
2 How many rooms are there?
3 Which rooms are there?
4 What don't they have?

> This is a houseboat. It has … . It doesn't have … .

5 🌟 Project Design a house.

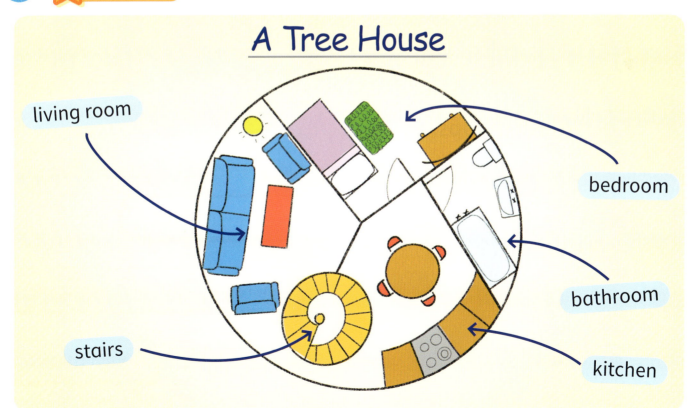

A Tree House

living room
bedroom
bathroom
kitchen
stairs

Geography

Do That!

1 🎧 90 Listen and act it out with your teacher. Then listen again and number the pictures.

2 Read the sentences from the story and draw lines.

a Open the window.

c Catch the spider.

e The spider waves goodbye.

b Put the spider outside.

d There's a big spider on the table.

f You're in the living room.

3 Work in groups.

a Make new sentences.

You're in the yard.
There's a ...
...

b Listen to a friend and act it out.

You're in the yard.

There's a little cat under a tree.

Touch the cat.

Group Check Units 5 and 6

1 How many words can you remember? Draw pictures or write words.

Days of the Week: MONDAY, TUESDAY

The House

2 Write and say the words.

3 🎧 91 Listen and number.

Yes, I do. ☐

That's great! ☐

In my living room. ☐

Do you play board games on the weekend? ☐

Where do you play them? ☐

4 🛡 Write a new dialogue. Act it out.

💬 Do you _____ on the weekend?

💬 Yes, I do.

💬 Where _____ ?

💬 In _____ .

💬 That's great!

Review 81

7 Get Dressed

1 🎧 92 Listen and look. Then listen and say the words.

1 sweater
2 skirt
3 shorts
4 pants
5 jacket
6 socks
7 jeans
8 shoes
9 baseball cap
10 T-shirt

BIG QUESTION How do clothes look different?

2 🎧 93 Listen and chant.

Put on your pants,
Put on your skirt,
Put on your sweater,
Put on your T-shirt.
Put on your shoes,
And your baseball cap.
Now let's rap!

Pants, T-shirt,
Shoes, and cap.
Sweater, skirt,
Now let's rap.

Come on Whisper,
It's time for school.

82 Clothes

1 🎧 94 **Listen, look, and draw lines.**

1 Do you like this T-shirt?
No, I don't.

2 Do you like these shoes?
Yes, I do.

2 ▶ 🎧 95 **Watch, listen, and say.**

Language Focus

Do you like these shoes?   Yes, **I do**.

Do you like this hat?   No, **I don't**.

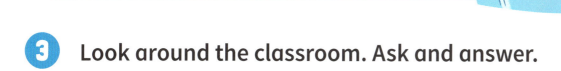

3 **Look around the classroom. Ask and answer.**

Do you like this bag?

Yes, I do.

Do you like this / these … ? 83

1 🎧 96 ▶ **Listen and sing. Then check ✓ the clothes in the song.**

Do you like this purple sweater?
Do you like this big blue hat?
Yes, I like your hat and sweater.
You look good like that.

**You look good, you look good,
You look good like that.
Socks and shoes, hats and caps,
You look good like that.**

Do you like these yellow pants?
Do you like this baseball cap?
Yes, I like your cap and pants.
You look good like that.

You look good, you look good ...

2 **Write a new verse for the song.**

Do you like _____?
Do you like _____?
Yes, I _____
You look good like that.

84 Singing for Pleasure

1 🎧 98 Listen and draw lines.

- David
- James
- Emily
- Gemma
- Katy
- Oliver

2 ▶ 🎧 99 Watch, listen, and say.

Language Focus

Look, that's Jim!
Is he wear**ing** a red hat?
No, he **isn't**.
Is he wear**ing** a blue hat?
Yes, he **is**. Jim's wear**ing** a blue hat.
Wave to him!

3 Look at Activity 1. Play the guessing game.

It's a girl.

Is she wearing a yellow T-shirt?

Yes, she is.

Is she … ?

Is he / she + ing?

The Cap

1   **Where's Whisper's cap?**

1

Whisper: My cap isn't here.
Flash: Oh, no!

2

Whisper: Look! Gary's wearing my cap.
Flash: Are you sure?
Misty: Maybe Gary has the same cap.

3
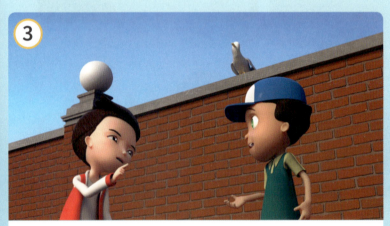
Whisper: Stop! That's my cap, Gary.
Gary: No, it's my cap.

4

Whisper: Get my cap, please.
Bird: No problem.

5

Gary: Hey!

6

Whisper: Thanks.

86 Value: Saying Sorry

Whisper: Oh, no! That's my cap!

Whisper: I'm very sorry, Gary.
Gary: It's OK.

2 Look at the picture and check ✓ the correct sentence.

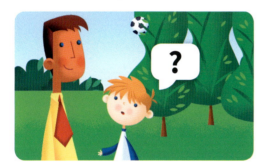

1 Oh, no! ☐
2 My jacket isn't here. ☐
3 Can you get my ball? ☐
4 She's wearing my T-shirt! ☐

Phonics

3 Find who says … **St**op!

4 🎧 101 Listen and say.

There are **st**ripes and dots on the socks on the **st**airs.

Phonics: The Letter Sounds *sp* and *st*

Skills

1 Read and write the numbers on the T-shirts.

1 May is wearing a yellow baseball cap, a blue T-shirt, and white socks.

2 Hugo is wearing a red baseball cap, a blue T-shirt, and white socks.

3 Lucy is wearing a yellow baseball cap, an orange T-shirt, and black socks.

4 Mike is wearing a red baseball cap, a green T-shirt, and purple socks.

5 Dan is wearing a white baseball cap, a green T-shirt, and black socks.

6 Jen is wearing a white baseball cap, an orange T-shirt, and purple socks.

1  Ask and answer.

"Is Tom riding a horse?" "No, I think he's riding a bike."

Tom: ride   Emma: play   Kylie: eat   Fred: play

2 🎧 102 Listen, check, and stick.

3 Choose an object and play the mime game.

"Are you eating a hot dog?" "Yes, I am."

4 Find a photo of your friend and write.

This is my friend Tom. He's wearing a blue sweater and blue pants.

Speaking, Listening, and Writing 89

Think and Learn

Patterns

▶ What patterns do you know?

1 Listen and point.

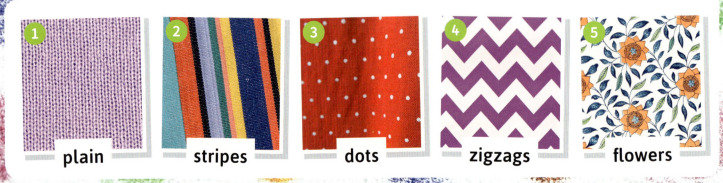

1 plain 2 stripes 3 dots 4 zigzags 5 flowers

2 Cover the photos in Activity 1. Ask and answer.

> What number are the dots?

> They're number …

3 Look and circle *yes* or *no*.

1 Does the jacket have dots? yes / no

2 Do the jeans have flowers? yes / no

3 Do the shoes have dots?  yes / no

4 Does the T-shirt have zigzags? yes / no

5 Does the skirt have flowers? yes / no

90 Art and Design

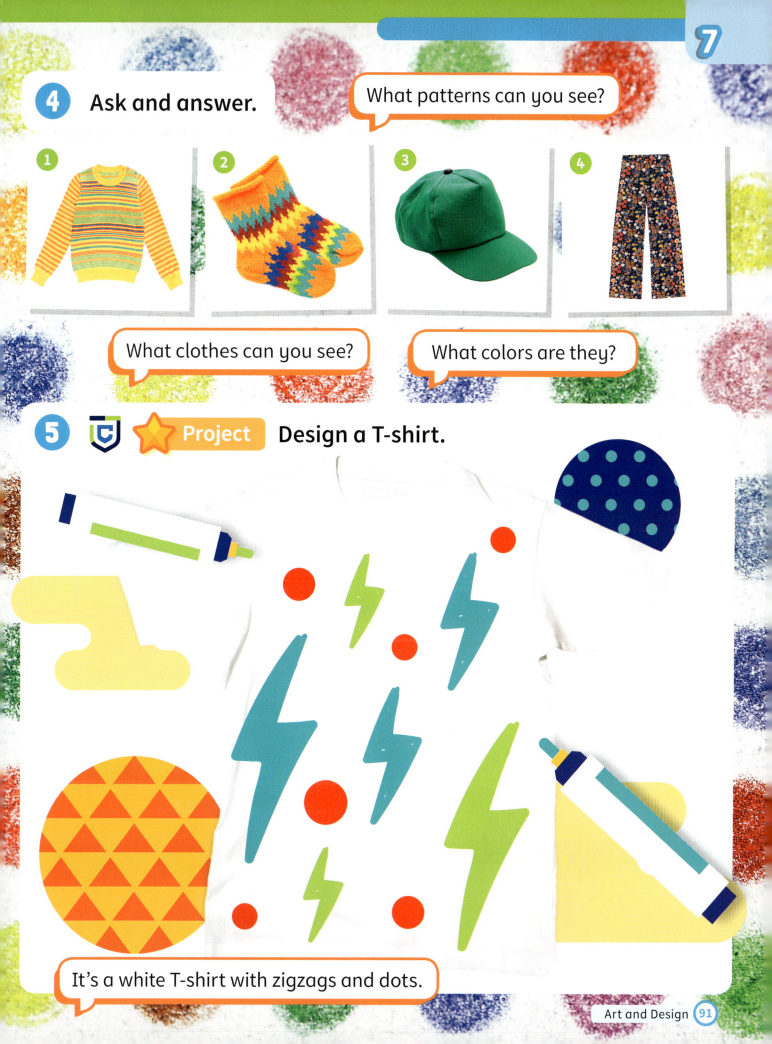

Create That!

1  Listen and imagine. Then draw your picture.

2 Work with a partner. Compare your pictures.

She's wearing …

He's wearing …

92 Creativity

Think Back 7

1 Read and circle.

1 This is a …
   a shirt. b skirt. c sweater.

2 These are …
   a shorts. b socks. c pants.

3 Do you like my baseball cap?
   a Yes, I do. b No, I don't.

4 Do you like these pants?
   a Yes, I do. b No, I don't.

5 Is Olivia wearing a red skirt?
   a Yes, she is. b No, she isn't.

6 Is Tim wearing a blue sweater?
   a Yes, he is. b No, he isn't.

7 In the story, Whisper's cap is …
   a orange. b blue. c red.

8 This T-shirt has …
   a dots. b stripes. c zigzags.

8 The Robot

1 🎧 105 Listen and look. Then listen and say the words.

1 arm
2 hand
3 knee
4 fingers
5 leg
6 foot
7 toes
8 head

 **BIG QUESTION** How can we move?

2 🎧 106 Listen and chant.

Let's make a robot.
You and me.
Here's a foot.
Here's a knee.

Here's an arm.
Here's a leg.
Here are the fingers.
Here's the head.

Here are the hands.
Here are the toes.
Let's make a robot.
Off it goes!

94 The Body

1 🎧 107 **Look and listen. What can Misty do?**

2 **Read and stick. Help the Super Friends see Misty.**

I can touch my toes.   I can skip.   I can stand on one leg.

3   **Watch, listen, and say.**

Language Focus

I **can** stand on one leg.   I **can** swim.
Go on—try it.   I **can** sing.
I **can** skip.   But I **can't** fly.

4 **Check** **or write an** ✗ **and say.**

A penguin can swim.

A penguin can't fly.

	swim	fly	walk
a penguin			
a fish			
a duck			

Can / Can't for Ability

1. 🎧 109 ▶ Listen and sing. Then look and draw lines.

I can take my foot
And put it on my head.
I can take my arm
And put it on my leg.

I can stick my tongue out,
And I can touch my nose.
I can take my right hand
And touch all of my toes.

I can cross my fingers,
And I can cross my knees.
But now I'm stuck. Oh, no!
Can you help me, please?

2. Read, think, and say. How are you the same as the boy in the song? What can you do?

I can take my arm and put it on my leg.

Singing for Pleasure; Help!

1 🎧 111 **Look and say. Then listen and check ✓ or put an ✗.**

Number 1 is play tennis.

play the piano   swim   ride a horse
ride a bike   play tennis   dance

Sophie

Tom

2 ▶ 🎧 112 **Watch, listen, and say.**

Language Focus

Can you cook?   **Can** you fly?
Yes, I **can**.   No, I **can't**.
Can you draw?   No, I **can't**.
No, I **can't**.   But I **can** dance!

3 **Ask and answer.**

Can you play tennis?

Yes, I can.

Questions with *Can* for Ability 97

The Problem

   When does Thunder touch his head?

Thunder: Give me the right leg and the left arm.
Whisper: Here's the right leg.
Flash: Here's the left arm.

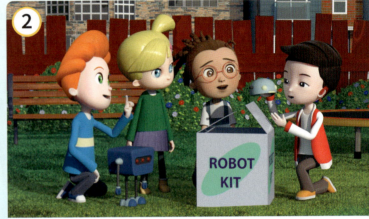

Thunder: And now the head, please.
Whisper: Here's the head.

Thunder: Batteries! We don't have batteries.
Flash: No problem.

Flash: Here you go.
Thunder: Thank you.

Thunder: Robot, can you speak?
Robot: nac I sey.

Whisper: We have a problem.
Thunder: It can't speak.
Misty: Let me try something.

Value: Teamwork

Whisper: What are you doing?
Misty: Robot, can you speak now?
Robot: Yes, I can.

Robot: Thank you, Misty.
Thunder: Good job, Misty.

2 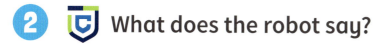 What does the robot say?

 koob

 smra

 toof

 ekib

 miws

Phonics

3 Find who says … *Give me the right leg.*

4 🎧 114 Listen and say.

Greg's got his fin**g**ers in a bi**g** **g**reen ba**g**.

Phonics: The Letter Sound *g*

Skills

1 🎧 115 **Listen and check ✓ the correct picture.**

1 Can Patch swim?

2 Can Sue ride a bike?

3 Can Coco stand on one leg?

2 **Play the find someone game.**

Can you …	Name
play chess?	
fly a kite?	
ride a horse?	
play the piano?	

Listening and Speaking

1 Read and match. Say the animal.

a. I have eight legs. I'm black with red dots. I can make webs. What am I?

b. I don't have arms or legs. I can't walk or run, but I can swim. What am I?

c. I have four legs. I'm big and brown. I can climb trees. What am I?

d. I have six legs, and I can fly. I can't walk well. What am I?

1 shark

2 bee

3 spider

4 bear

2 Draw and write about an animal.

My Animal Project
I have two legs.
I'm black and white,
and I can't fly.
What am I?

I'm a penguin.

Reading and Writing

Think and Learn
Movements

▶ How do you move?

1 🎧 116 Listen and point.

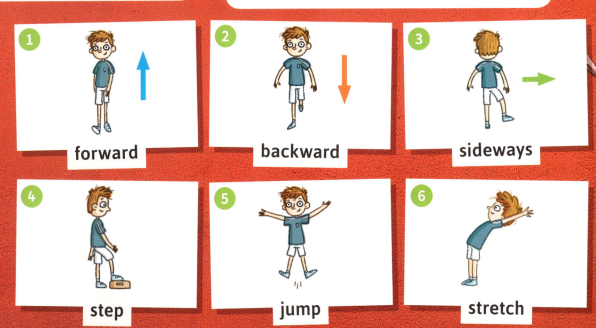

1. forward
2. backward
3. sideways
4. step
5. jump
6. stretch

2 🎧 117 Listen and do the movements.

3 Look and say.

go forward ↑   go backward ↓
go sideways to the left ←   go sideways to the right →   steps 👣

1 **4** 👣 ↑ and then **5** 👣 →

2 **3** 👣 ↓ and then **2** 👣 ←

3 **1** 👣 ↑ and then **1** 👣 ↓

4 **2** 👣 ← and then **6** 👣 ↑

> Go four steps forward and then five steps sideways to your right.

102 Physical Education

4 Read and write the numbers.

☐ She stretches her legs. ☐ She stretches backward.
☐ She jumps. ☐ She stretches her arms forward.

5 Project — Make a dance. Show your friends.

Stretch your arms.

Stretch your legs.

Go sideways.

Jump.

Physical Education

Do That!

1 🎧 118 Listen and act it out with your teacher. Then listen again and number the pictures.

2 Read the sentences from the story and draw lines.

a Bounce your ball.

b The ball is in a tree.

c Throw your ball in the sky.

d Where is the ball?

e You have a big ball.

f Oh, no!

3 🛡 Work in groups.

a Make new sentences.

> You have a small plane.
> Throw ... in the sky.
> ... is ...

b Listen to a friend and act it out.

> You have a small plane.
> Throw your plane in the sky.
> Your plane is in the water.

Creativity

Group Check Units 7 and 8

1 How many words can you remember? Draw pictures.

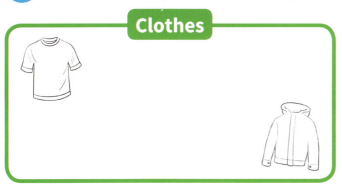

Clothes

The Body

2 Write and say the words.

3 🎧 119 Listen and number.

Yes, he is. ☐

He's over there. ☐

Can you see Luke? ☐

Is he wearing jeans? ☐

No, I can't. Which boy is he? ☐

4 Write a new dialogue. Act it out.

💬 Can you see _____ ?

💬 No, I can't. Which _____ ?

💬 _____ over there.

💬 Is _____ ?

💬 Yes, _____ is.

Review 105

9 At the Beach

1 🎧 120 **Listen and look. Then listen and say the words.**

1. paint a picture
2. listen to music
3. catch a fish
4. take a photo
5. eat ice cream
6. play the guitar
7. read a book
8. make a sandcastle
9. look for shells

BIG QUESTION Where can we go on vacation?

2 🎧 121 **Listen and chant.**

Eat ice cream,
Yum, yum.
Take a photo,
Click, click.
Catch a fish,
Splash, splish.

Make a sandcastle,
Dig, dig.
Look for shells,
Look, look.
Play in the sun.
It's lots of fun!

106 Vacations

1. 🎧 122 **Listen and number the pictures. Then write.**

paint   take   look   listen

Let's _____ to music.
Good idea.

Let's _____ a picture.
I'm not sure.

Let's _____ for shells.
Sorry, I don't want to.

Let's _____ a picture.
Good idea.

2. ▶ 🎧 123 **Watch, listen, and say.**

Language Focus

Let's eat ice cream.
I'm not sure.
Let's listen to music.
Sorry, I don't want to.

Let's play the guitar.
Good idea.
Let's listen to music
and **play** the guitar.

3. **Look and act out.**

Let's …
Good idea.

Suggestions 107

Listen and sing. Then number the pictures.

Let's go to the mountains
And climb a tree.
Let's take some photos,
You and me.

**Vacation, vacation,
Vacation time is near.
Vacation, vacation,
The end of the year!**

Let's go to the beach
And swim in the ocean.
Let's catch a fish,
You and me.

Vacation, vacation ...

No! Let's stay at home
And watch TV.
Let's play and talk,
Just you and me.

Vacation, vacation ...

2 **Plan a perfect vacation.**

Let's go to the mountains.

No, let's stay at home. It's too cold.

1 🎧 126 Listen and read. Check ✓ the correct picture.

1 Where's the shell?

2 Where are the kites?

2 ▶ 🎧 127 Watch, listen, and say.

Language Focus

Where **are** my sunglasses?   Where**'s** my hat?
They aren't in my bag.   **It isn't** in my bag.
They aren't in the box.   **It isn't** in the box.
They aren't on the rocks.   **It isn't** on the rocks.
They're on my head!   **It's** on my head!

3 Play the question game.

Where's … ?

It's …

Where's / Where are … ? 109

The Top of the Hill

  What does Thunder have in picture 7?

Whisper and Misty: A race?
Flash: Yes! Let's go.

Flash: Bye. See you at the top of the hill!

Whisper: A race is not a good idea.
Misty: I can walk up the hill, but I can't run!
Thunder: Just wait and see.

Flash: What's that? … Oh, no!

Flash: This is the end of the race. We can't get to the top of the hill.

Thunder: Let me try.
Flash: Thanks, Thunder.

110 Value: Modesty

Thunder: Now you can race to the top, Flash!
Flash: No. Let's go together. That's more fun!

Misty: What a good idea!
Whisper: Yes!

2 Read, think, and write the names.

1 I'm super! _____
2 A race? I'm not happy about that. _____
3 Flash can't see it. _____
4 I really like my friends. _____

Phonics

3 Find who says …   Just wait and s**ee**.

4 🎧 129   Listen and say.

J**ea**n **ea**ts ice cr**ea**m under a tr**ee** on the b**ea**ch.

Phonics: The Letter Sounds *ee* and *ea*

Skills

1   Listen and stick.

2 Look at Activity 1 again. Make sentences.

> The ice cream is …

112 Listening and Speaking

1 Read and write the country.

Come to the USA

Go to a National Park. Look at the beautiful old trees. Catch a fish in a lake. Sleep in a tent under the stars.

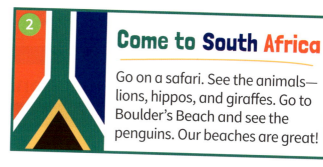

Come to South Africa

Go on a safari. See the animals—lions, hippos, and giraffes. Go to Boulder's Beach and see the penguins. Our beaches are great!

a _____

b _____

2 🎧 131 Listen and check ✓ the country.

	1	2	3	4	5
USA					
South Africa					

3 Make a poster about your country.

Come to Mexico. See the beautiful beaches and swim in the ocean.

Reading, Listening, and Writing

Think and Learn

Landscapes

▶ What can we do on vacation?

1 🎧 132 Listen and point.

1. mountains
2. country
3. beach
4. city
5. theme park
6. campsite
7. lake

2 Read and say.

> We can swim here.

> The beach.

> The lake.

1 We can swim here.
2 We can see plants and animals here.
3 We can look for shells here.
4 We can eat ice cream and ride on fun things here.
5 We can go to stores here.
6 We can sleep in a tent here.

3 Ask and answer.

> What can you do on vacation at home?

> I can swim and I can ride my bike.

4 Read and match.

a mountains

b beach

c lake

d campsite

e city

f country

1 Take a tent and go on vacation.
2 Climb up and see the view.
3 Make a sandcastle and go surfing.
4 Ride bikes and see lots of trees.
5 Go on a boat and catch a fish.
6 Take photos and have a pizza.

5    Make a calendar for a perfect vacation.

Monday	Tuesday	Wednesday	Thursday	Friday
Take the train.	Go to the beach.	Eat ice cream.	Go on a boat.	Go home.

Geography 115

Create That!

1 🎧 133 Listen and imagine. Then draw your picture.

2 Work with a partner. Compare your pictures.

> I can ... on my vacation.

> You can ... on your vacation.

Creativity

Think Back 9

1 Read and circle.

1 I can ... a sandcastle.
   a eat   b play   c make

2 I can ... a photo.
   a take   b look for   c read

3 Let's ...
   a catch a fish.   b paint a picture.   c listen to music.

4 Let's ...
   a read a book.   b eat ice cream.   c play the guitar.

5 Where ... the shells?
   a is   b are

6 Where ... the kite?
   a is   b are

7 In the story, ... wants a race.
   a Flash   b Thunder   c Misty

8 We are at the ...
   a campsite.   b lake.   c theme park.

Review 117

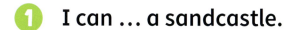

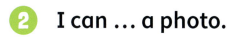

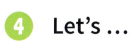

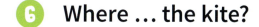

Friends

Numbers

1 Look and match.   1 3 5 7 8 10   How old are you?

1 I'm seven.
2 I'm three.
3 I'm one.
4 I'm eight.
5 I'm five.
6 I'm ten.

Colors

2 Look and write the colors.

1 d r e   _ _ _
2 l u e b   _ _ _ _
3 n e r e g _ _ _ _ _
4 w l o l y e _ _ _ _ _ _
5 r e n g o a _ _ _ _ _ _
6 r u p p e l _ _ _ _ _ _

Friends: Language Focus

1 At School

Questions and Short Answers

What's this? What's this?

Is it a pencil?   **Is it a** ruler?
No, **it isn't**.   Yes, **it is**.

1 Write questions and answers.

1 this / ? / What's

_____

2 a / it / ? / Is / bag

_____

3 pencil / this / a /? / Is

_____

book / It's / a / .

_____

isn't / it / . / No,

_____

it / . / Yes, / is

_____

Imperatives

Sit at your desk, please.   **Open** your book, please.
Now **get** a pen.   **Write** one to ten.

2 Complete the sentences with words from the box.

1 _____ your pencil case, please.
2 _____ some paper, please.
3 _____ in your notebook, please.
4 _____ me an eraser, please.

| Pass |
| Close |
| Write |
| Get |

Unit 1: Language Focus 119

2 Let's Play

What's his / her … ? How old is he / she?

What's **his** name?
His name's Ben.
How old is **he**?
He's ten.
What's **his** favorite toy?
His favorite toy's **his** train.

What's **her** name?
Her name's Kate.
How old is **she**?
She's eight.
What's **her** favorite toy?
Her favorite toy's **her** plane.

1 Read and draw lines.

1 What's his name?
2 How old is he?
3 What's her name?
4 How old is she?

a She's seven.
b Her name's Sara.
c His name's Sam.
d He's eight.

Adjectives

It's a **white** ball.
It's a **big white** ball.

It's an **ugly** ball.
And it's **cold**.

2 Write the words in order.

1	long	a	train	blue	_____
2	kite	yellow	a	new	_____
3	small	monster	green	a	_____
4	go-kart	an	old	red	_____

3 Pet Show

Prepositions: *in, on, under*

The frog's **in** my bag.
It's **under** my chair.
The frog's **on** my hat.
It's really there.

My frog? Where is it?
It's not **in** my bag.
It's not **under** my chair.
It's not **on** my hat.
It isn't there.

1 Look, match, and write *in*, *on*, and *under*.

1 The rat is _____ the desk. ☐
2 The frog is _____ the bag. ☐
3 The lizard is _____ the pencil case. ☐
4 The cat is _____ the book. ☐

I like / I don't like …

I **like** frogs.
What about you?
I **like** frogs, too.

Croak, croak!
I **don't like big** frogs!
Croak. Croak!

2 Look, read, and circle.

1 ✓ I **like** / **don't like** dogs.
2 ✗ I **like** / **don't like** rats.
3 ✓ I **like** / **don't like** donkeys.
4 ✗ I **like** / **don't like** lizards.

Unit 3: Language Focus 121

4 Lunchtime

I have / I don't have ...

I **have** a carrot.
I **have** a carrot.
Look what I can do.

Oh, go away,
You silly parrot.
Now I **don't have** a carrot!

1 Look and write.

1 I ✓ _____ a cheese sandwich and an apple. I ✗ _____ a cake.
2 I ✓ _____ a cheese sandwich and a cake. I ✗ _____ an apple.
3 I ✓ _____ an apple and a cake. I ✗ _____ a cheese sandwich.
4 I ✓ _____ a cheese sandwich, an apple, and a cake.

Do ... have any ... ?

Penny, I'm hungry.
Do we **have any** fish?
No, we **don't**.
We don't have any fish.

Penny, I'm hungry.
Do we **have any** fish?
Yes, we **do**!
Yes, we have a fish!

2 Look, read, and check.

1 Do we have any pizza?   ✓   Yes, we do. ☐   No, we don't. ☐
2 Do we have any sausages? ✗   Yes, we do. ☐   No, we don't. ☐
3 Do we have any steaks?   ✗   Yes, we do. ☐   No, we don't. ☐
4 Do we have any fish?   ✓   Yes, we do. ☐   No, we don't. ☐

5 Free Time

I (watch TV) on (Sundays).

I **go swimming** on Mondays,
Swimming in the ocean.
I **play soccer** on Tuesdays.
Come and play with me!

I **go fishing** on Wednesdays,
And Thursdays and Fridays, too.
But on Saturdays and Sundays,
I like **being** with you.

1 Read and circle.

1 I **do** / **play** the piano on Mondays.
2 I **play** / **ride** my horse on Tuesdays.
3 I **go** / **do** swimming on Wednesdays.
4 I **play** / **go** computer games on Saturdays.
5 I **do** / **ride** my bike on Sundays.

Do you … ? Yes, I do. / No, I don't.

Do you watch TV on the weekend?
No, I **don't**.
Do you play computer games?
Yes, I **do**.

Do you ride your horse on the weekend?
No, I **don't**.
Do you ride your bike with Paul?
Yes, I **do**.

2 Look, read, and write.

1 Do you _____ soccer on Mondays?   ✗   _____, I _____.
2 Do you _____ in the park on Wednesdays?   ✓   _____, I _____.
3 Do you _____ fishing on Fridays?   ✓   _____, I _____.
4 Do you _____ TV on the weekend?   ✗   _____, I _____.

Unit 5: Language Focus 123

6 The Old House

There's ... / There are ...

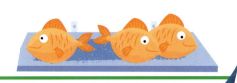

There's a fish in the hall
And two fish in the living room.

There are three fish in the kitchen.
There are four fish in the dining room.

1 Look and write *There is* or *There are*.

1 _____ a lizard in the hall.
2 _____ a ball in the basement.
3 _____ three cats in the living room.
4 _____ a frog in the bathroom.
5 _____ six apples in the kitchen.

Is / Are there ... ? How many ... ?

Is there a park?
No, **there isn't**.
Is there a school?
Yes, **there is**.

Are there any trees?
No, **there aren't**.
Are there any houses?
Yes, **there are**.

How many are there?

2 Look and write. Then draw lines.

Is Are How many

1 _____ there any children in the park?
2 _____ trees are there in the yard?
3 _____ there a spider in the bathroom?

a Yes, there is.
b No, there aren't.
c There are three.

Unit 6: Language Focus

7 Get Dressed

Do you like this / these … ?

Do you like these shoes?   Yes, **I do**.

Do you like this hat?   No, **I don't**.

1 Read and circle.

1 Do you like **this** / **these** T-shirt?
2 Do you like **this** / **these** shorts?
3 Do you like **this** / **these** jeans?
4 Do you like **this** / **these** jacket?

5 Do you like this baseball cap?
No, I **do** / **don't**.
6 Do you like these socks?
Yes, I **do** / **don't**.

Is he / she + ing?

Look, that's Jim!
Is he wear**ing** a red hat?
No, he **isn't**.
Is he wear**ing** a blue hat?
Yes, he **is**. Jim's wear**ing** a blue hat.
Wave to him!

2 Write the questions and sentences.

1 Tom / jeans / wearing / is / . _____
2 Tim / Is / wearing / a / jacket / ? _____
3 Joe and Zoe / shoes / wearing / Are / ? _____
4 Dan and Ann / jackets / red / wearing / are / . _____

8 The Robot

Can / Can't for Ability

I **can** stand on one leg.
Go on—try it.
I **can** skip.

I **can** swim.
I **can** sing.
But I **can't** fly.

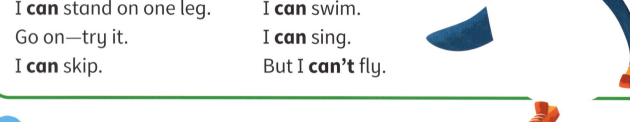

1 Look and write.

	Lucy	Alex
skip	✓	✗
swim	✗	✗
dance	✓	✓

1 _____
2 _____
3 _____
4 _____
5 _____
6 _____

Questions with Can for Ability

Can you cook?
Yes, I **can**.
Can you draw?
No, I **can't**.

Can you fly?
No, I **can't**.
No, I **can't**.
But I **can** dance!

2 Complete with words from the box.   [Yes   can't   But   Can]

Bill: Hi, Jill. ¹_____ you play the guitar?

Jill: No, I ²_____. ³_____ I can sing and dance.

Bill: And can you play the piano?

Jill: ⁴_____, I can.

9 At the Beach

Suggestions

Let's eat ice cream.
I'm not sure.
Let's listen to music.
Sorry, I don't want to.

Let's play the guitar.
Good idea.
Let's listen to music
and **play** the guitar.

1 Look and write.

| sure   want   Let's   build   Sorry |

Anna: ¹ _____ catch a fish!
Nick: I'm not ² _____.
Anna: OK. Let's ³ _____ a sandcastle.

Nick: ⁴ _____, I don't ⁵ _____ to.
Anna: OK. Let's eat ice cream!

Where's / Where are … ?

Where **are** my sunglasses?
They aren't in my bag.
They aren't in the box.
They aren't on the rocks.
They're on my head!

Where**'s** my hat?
It isn't in my bag.
It isn't in the box.
It isn't on the rocks.
It's on my head!

2 Write the questions and answers.

1 are / Where / shells / the / ?   _____
2 the / beach / They / on / are / .   _____
3 is / the / Where / fish / ?   _____
4 ocean / in / It's / the / .   _____

Unit 9: Language Focus 127

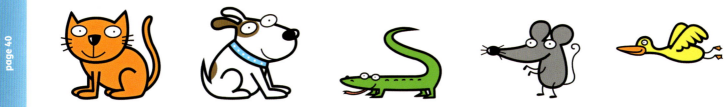

There are seven.   No, there aren't.

Yes, there are.   Yes, there is.